KATY TRAIL

TRAVEL GUIDE 2024-2025

Your Essential Companion to Exploring Scenic Paths, Historical Landmarks, and Authentic Local Flavors across Missouri's Wine Country and beyond.

Cedric J. Stone

COPYRIGHT

Table of Contents

Gratitude

Dear Readers,

Thank you for choosing this book to guide you on your next adventure. Your interest and curiosity are greatly appreciated, and I am grateful for the chance to share the beauties of our world with you. Before you begin the adventures detailed within these pages, I'd like to express my heartfelt gratitude.

Your support means everything to me, and I am confident that this book will be a valuable companion on your journey. Whether you're planning your first vacation or returning to uncover new treasures, you'll find inspiration, practical insights, and a greater bond with the places you visit.

Enjoy every second of your journey, and may your memories be as breathtaking as the sights you will see.

Thank you for your participation in our adventure.

KATY TRAIL, MISSOURI MAP

SCAN ME

HOW TO SCAN THE QR CODE

1. Open your smartphone's camera or QR code scanner app.
2. Point the camera at the QR code.
3. Wait for the camera to recognize the code.
4. Tap the notification or link that appears.
5. Follow the link or instructions provided.

INTRODUCTION

Welcome to the Katy Trail

Nestled in the heart of Missouri, the Katy Trail offers a captivating blend of natural beauty, rich history, and vibrant culture. Spanning 237 miles along the banks of the Missouri River, this remarkable trail is one of the longest rail-trails in the United States, transforming an old railway line into a scenic pathway for hikers, cyclists, and nature enthusiasts alike. Whether you're seeking an exhilarating adventure or a peaceful retreat, the Katy Trail invites you to explore its diverse landscapes, charming towns, and warm communities.

The Katy Trail at a Glance

The Katy Trail stretches from St. Charles in the east to Clinton in the west, winding through picturesque small towns, lush forests, and rolling hills. As you traverse the trail, you'll encounter a variety of ecosystems, including wetlands, prairies, and river bluffs. This diversity makes the Katy Trail a haven for outdoor activities, offering ample opportunities for hiking, biking, birdwatching, and photography. The trail is also dotted with historical landmarks, wineries, and local eateries, making it a perfect destination for those looking to immerse themselves in Missouri's culture.

History and Significance of the Trail

The Katy Trail is steeped in history, originating from the Missouri-Kansas-Texas Railroad, known as the "Katy". The railroad, which began operations in the late 1800s, played a crucial role in connecting Missouri with Texas and facilitating the movement of goods and people. However, with the rise of the automobile and changing transportation patterns, the railroad ceased operations in the 1980s.

In 1988, recognizing the potential of this abandoned railway line, the state of Missouri began converting it into a recreational trail. Officially opened in 1990, the Katy Trail quickly gained popularity among outdoor enthusiasts and has since become a beloved destination for both locals and tourists. Today, it stands as a testament to the importance of preserving our natural and historical resources while promoting outdoor recreation.

A Personal Journey

The Katy Trail isn't just a destination; it's a journey that connects you with the essence of Missouri. Each mile brings something new—whether it's the laughter of fellow cyclists, the stunning vistas over the Missouri River, or the warm hospitality of small-town locals. The trail serves as a backdrop for personal adventures and shared memories, allowing you to escape the hustle and bustle of daily life and reconnect with nature and yourself.

Whether you're an experienced hiker or a casual day-tripper, the Katy Trail welcomes all. The trail is accessible year-round, making it an ideal destination in every season. In spring, vibrant wildflowers bloom, painting the landscape with color; summer offers lush greenery and abundant wildlife; autumn presents a stunning display of fall foliage; and winter transforms the trail into a serene, snow-covered wonderland.

Why Visit the Katy Trail in 2024-2025

The Katy Trail offers a one-of-a-kind experience for outdoor enthusiasts, history lovers, and travelers alike, making 2024-2025 the perfect time to explore this iconic rail-trail. Stretching 237 miles across Missouri, the Katy Trail is the longest developed rail-trail in the United States, providing visitors with stunning views of the Missouri River, lush forests, farmland, and historic towns. As one of the state's most beloved outdoor destinations, it promises a mix of adventure, tranquility, and discovery.

In 2024-2025, the trail's appeal is enhanced by recent upgrades to trailheads, signage, and accommodations, ensuring an even more enjoyable journey for both first-time visitors and returning explorers. Seasonal events, such as Hermann's Oktoberfest and the Missouri State Fair, offer opportunities to experience Missouri's rich culture, local food, and vibrant community life, making the trail much more than just a scenic path.

Whether you're cycling through wine country, hiking along river bluffs, or simply taking in the beauty of autumn foliage, the Katy Trail is the perfect setting for those looking to escape into nature while still engaging with local culture and history. The trail also promotes sustainable travel, allowing visitors to enjoy a low-impact adventure while supporting small businesses in charming towns like St. Charles, Rocheport, and Boonville.

With its accessibility, diverse landscapes, and endless opportunities for adventure, the Katy Trail in 2024-2025 offers an unforgettable experience for anyone seeking to connect with nature, history, and Missouri's heartland.

How to Use This Guide

This guide has been designed to be your comprehensive companion for exploring the Katy Trail, whether you're a first-time visitor or a seasoned traveler returning to enjoy new discoveries. Organized into clear, easy-to-navigate chapters, this guide covers everything from the trail's historical significance and scenic wonders to the best accommodations, food, and cultural events you'll encounter along the way. Each section is tailored to provide the most relevant and practical information to help you make the most of your adventure on the trail.

To begin, the "Introduction" section offers a warm welcome to the Katy Trail and dives into its history, significance, and highlights for 2024-2025. For those new to the trail, this section provides context for why the Katy Trail is a must-visit destination. If you're looking to get a sense of what to expect throughout the year, the "Planning Your Trip" chapter covers important information like the best times to visit, how to prepare, and advice on transportation and accommodations.

As you dive deeper into your journey, the "Practical Information" chapter is your go-to resource for understanding the trail itself—trailheads, maps, safety tips, and essential rules to follow while exploring. If you're curious about the different regions and what makes each unique, head over to the "Regions of the Katy Trail" chapter, which breaks down the trail's Eastern, Central, and Western sections, offering insights on must-see spots in each area.

For adventurers looking to combine trail time with culture, the chapters on "Top Landmarks" and "Festivals and Events" will guide you to the best places to visit and local celebrations you won't want to miss. For those who seek a more immersive outdoor experience, chapters on "Outdoor Adventure", "Accommodations", and "Food and Drink" will help you find everything from cozy B&Bs to local eateries and Missouri's renowned wineries.

To plan your trip based on your schedule and interests, consult the "Suggested Itineraries" chapter for tailored recommendations, whether you're planning a one-day outing or a week-long journey. And for the environmentally conscious, the "Sustainable and Responsible Travel" chapter offers tips on minimizing your impact while supporting local communities.

As you set out to discover the wonders of the Katy Trail, remember: every journey begins with a single step. So, let the trail lead you into the heart of Missouri's enchanting landscapes, where adventure and discovery await at every turn. Welcome to the Katy Trail—your adventure starts here!

CHAPTER ONE

Planning Your Trip

Planning a trip to the Katy Trail can be a delightful experience, but it requires some forethought to ensure you make the most of your adventure. With its stunning landscapes, diverse activities, and charming towns, the Katy Trail offers something for everyone. This chapter will guide you through essential considerations, helping you create a memorable journey filled with fun and exploration.

Best Time to Visit the Katy Trail

Choosing the right time to visit the Katy Trail is crucial for enjoying the best of what it has to offer. Generally, the trail is open year-round, but each season presents its own unique charm. Below is a closer look on this:

Spring (March to May)

As winter melts away, the Katy Trail bursts into life with vibrant wildflowers and fresh greenery. This is a great time for birdwatching, as many migratory birds return to the area. Spring also hosts several local events and festivals that showcase the region's culture.

Summer (June to August)

Summer offers long days and warm weather, ideal for biking and hiking. However, be prepared for heat, especially in July and August. Early mornings or late afternoons are the best times for outdoor activities to avoid the peak sun. This season also sees an increase in local farmers' markets, where you can sample fresh produce and local specialties.

Fall (September to November)

Autumn is one of the most popular periods to visit the Katy Trail. This season is perfect for leisurely bike rides and hikes as the weather cools down. Fall festivals, harvest events, and wine tastings are abundant, allowing visitors to experience the local culture.

Winter (December to February)

Winter brings a quieter atmosphere to the Katy Trail. While snow can blanket the landscape, making it picturesque, it may limit some outdoor activities. However, if you enjoy solitude and peaceful surroundings, winter hiking or cross-country skiing can be rewarding experiences. Many towns along the trail also host holiday events and activities.

Preparing for the Journey

Once you've decided on your travel dates, it's time to get into the nitty-gritty aspect of trip planning Here are key considerations to help you prepare for your adventure on the Katy Trail:

Physical Preparation

While the Katy Trail is accessible to people of all fitness levels, it's wise to prepare physically, especially if you plan on biking long distances. If you're new to biking or hiking, consider starting with shorter walks or rides before your trip. If you're an experienced outdoor enthusiast, aim for longer and more challenging routes to gauge your stamina.

Packing Essentials

Your packing list will vary depending on the season and your chosen activities, but here are some essentials to consider:

- **Clothing:** Wear moisture-wicking, breathable fabrics, and layers for temperature changes. A good pair of hiking or biking shoes is essential, along with a hat and sunglasses for sun protection.

- **Hydration:** Carry a refillable water bottle or hydration pack to stay hydrated on the trail.

There are several water sources along the route, but it's best to have your own supply.

- **Snacks:** Pack energy-boosting snacks like nuts, granola bars, and fruit for your journey. This will keep you fueled during your hikes or rides.

- **Navigation Tools:** Although the trail is well-marked, a map or a reliable GPS app can enhance your navigation experience.

- **First Aid Kit:** A basic first aid kit is a good idea for any outdoor adventure. Include items like antiseptic wipes and pain relievers.

- **Sun Protection:** Sunscreen, lip balm with SPF, and insect repellent are essential, especially during warmer months.

Booking Accommodations

The Katy Trail is lined with charming towns, each offering a variety of accommodation options. The following are some things to consider when booking your stay:

- **Location:** Choose a lodging option based on your planned trail segments. Staying close to a trailhead or in a town that offers easy access to the trail can save travel time.

- **Type of Accommodation:** Options range from hotels and motels to bed-and-breakfasts and campgrounds. Each offers a unique experience, so choose one that suits your preferences.

- **Amenities:** Look for accommodations that provide bike storage, laundry facilities, and breakfast options, especially if you plan on cycling long distances.

Transportation Options

Getting to the Katy Trail and navigating around it is an important aspect of your trip planning. The following are the available transportation options to consider:

- **Arriving by Car:** Most visitors drive to the Katy Trail. The trail is accessible from several major highways, and parking is available at various trailheads. Renting a car is also an option if you're flying into Missouri.

- **Public Transportation:** If you're traveling from out of state, consider taking a bus or train to a nearby city, such as St. Louis or Kansas City, and then renting a car or using local shuttle services to reach the trail.

- **Bike Rentals and Shuttle Services:** Several towns along the trail offer bike rentals, making it easy for visitors to explore without bringing their bikes. Shuttle services are also available for transporting you and your bike between towns, making it convenient to plan a multi-day trip without backtracking.

Weather and Seasonal Considerations

Missouri's weather can be unpredictable, so it's wise to check the forecast before you go. Here's what to expect in each season:

- **Spring:** Temperatures range from the 50s to the 70s °F (10-25°C), but be prepared for rain. A lightweight rain jacket is essential.

- **Summer:** Expect temperatures between the 70s and 90s °F (20-35°C). Stay hydrated and beware of heat stroke.

- **Fall:** Temperatures can vary widely, from the 50s to the 70s °F (10-25°C). Layering is a prime factor in adapting to changing conditions.

- **Winter:** Expect chilly temperatures, often in the 20s and 30s °F (-6 to 3°C). Snow is possible, so dress warmly and plan for winter conditions.

Visa and Entry Requirements

For international travelers, it's essential to check visa and entry requirements well in advance. Most visitors from countries in the Visa Waiver Program can enter the U.S. for tourism for up to 90 days without a visa. However, travelers from other countries may need to apply for a visa. Always carry a valid passport and any necessary documentation when traveling.

With careful planning, your trip to the Katy Trail can be an unforgettable adventure. Whether you're seeking thrilling outdoor activities, a peaceful retreat in nature, or an exploration of local culture, this trail offers an unparalleled experience. By considering the best time to visit, preparing physically, and making necessary arrangements, you can ensure a fulfilling journey along this iconic trail.

So, gear up, gather your travel companions, and get ready to discover the beauty and charm of the Katy Trail in 2024-2025! Adventure awaits!

CHAPTER TWO

Practical Information

Planning a trip to the Katy Trail requires more than just deciding where to start and what sights to see. Knowing the ins and outs of practical details can make the difference between a smooth, enjoyable journey and one fraught with preventable hiccups. In this chapter, we'll cover essential practical information you'll need to ensure your Katy Trail adventure is as seamless as possible. From safety tips to navigation, we've got you covered with up-to-date details for 2024-2025.

Navigating the Trail: Trailheads, Maps, and Signage

The Katy Trail is well-marked and maintained, making navigation straightforward. However, having a solid grasp of the trailheads, maps, and signage will significantly improve your experience. Below is a closer look is at this aspect:

Trailheads

There are over 30 trailheads along the Katy Trail, each serving as convenient starting points for cyclists, hikers, and walkers. Major trailheads include St. Charles, Rocheport, Jefferson City, Hermann, and Clinton, with others scattered along the route. Each trailhead provides parking and is equipped with informational boards, restrooms, and in some cases, water stations. For those planning multi-day journeys, trailheads also serve as excellent points to plan overnight stops, whether you're staying at a local inn or camping nearby.

Maps
While the Katy Trail is straightforward, carrying a map or having a GPS app is advisable. Maps can be picked up at visitor centers or downloaded from various online resources. Many local apps provide interactive trail maps that allow users to track their progress, find nearby attractions, and even estimate the distance between towns and services. These tools are especially helpful for planning breaks, overnight stops, or detours to interesting spots off the main trail.

Signage

Clear signage along the trail ensures visitors know where they are at all times. Mileage markers are placed every mile along the trail, which helps travelers gauge their progress and plan for stops. Directional signs to nearby towns and amenities such as restrooms, water stations, and bike repair shops are easy to spot, and informational plaques are scattered along the trail to provide historical and environmental context.

Safety Tips for the Trail

Safety should be of utmost importance when embarking on any outdoor adventure. Although the Katy Trail is generally safe, taking a few precautions will help you avoid potential issues.

General Safety

- **Stay on the Trail:** The Katy Trail passes through some remote areas, so it's essential to stay on the designated path. Venturing off-trail can lead to dangerous situations, especially in dense wooded areas or near water.

- **Buddy System:** If possible, travel with a friend or group, especially if you're planning to traverse longer stretches of the trail. While solo travel is entirely safe for most of the year, having someone with you provides an extra layer of security.

- **Emergency Contacts**: Save local emergency numbers in your phone and share your itinerary with someone back home. Having a plan for checking in can help ease concerns, especially on longer trips.

- **Wildlife Awareness:** The trail is home to various wildlife, including deer, raccoons, and occasionally, snakes. While these animals tend to avoid humans, be mindful of your surroundings, especially in more remote areas.

Rules and Regulations for Trail Use

While the Katy Trail is open to the public and welcomes visitors year-round, there are some guidelines that ensure the trail remains safe and enjoyable for everyone.

- **Hours of Operation:** The Katy Trail is open from sunrise to sunset. Visitors are encouraged to plan their trips within daylight hours for safety and to respect local regulations.

- **Motorized Vehicles:** Motorized vehicles are not allowed on the trail, except for official park services. The trail is reserved for non-motorized transportation such as biking, hiking, and horseback riding in designated areas.

- **Pets:** Pets are welcome on the trail but must be kept on a leash at all times. Be mindful of other trail users and clean up after your pet to keep the trail enjoyable for all.

- **Littering:** Keep the trail clean by packing out everything you bring in. Many trailheads have waste disposal areas, so use them to properly dispose of trash.

- **Respect for Others:** The Katy Trail is a shared space, so always be courteous to fellow travelers. If you're biking, signal when you're passing pedestrians, and keep to the right to allow others to pass.

Essential Items to Pack for Hiking or Biking

Proper preparation is key to a successful trip on the Katy Trail. Whether you're out for a day hike or a multi-day biking excursion, packing the right gear ensures you're ready for anything the trail throws your way.

Day Trip Essentials

For shorter trips, pack light but cover your basics:

- **Water:** At least one liter of water per hour of activity.
- **Snacks:** High-energy snacks such as granola bars, fruit, or trail mix.
- **Clothing:** Moisture-wicking clothing, a hat, and sunglasses for sun protection.
- **First Aid Kit:** Basic first aid supplies.
- **Navigation Tools:** A map or GPS app for tracking your route.

- **Multi-tool or Bike Repair Kit:** If biking, be sure to bring a small toolset for minor repairs.
- **Phone and Charger:** While some stretches of the trail may not have great cell service, it's important to keep your phone charged in case of emergencies.

Multi-Day Trip Essentials

If you're planning to spend several days on the trail, you'll need to carry more gear:

- **Camping Equipment:** A lightweight tent or sleeping bag if camping along the trail.
- **Extra Clothing:** A change of clothes, especially if weather conditions are variable.
- **Food:** Enough meals for your journey, as some towns along the trail have limited dining options.
- **Portable Power Bank:** To keep your electronics charged, especially if camping.

- **Bike Tools and Spare Tubes:** For cyclists, pack an extra tube and patch kit in case of punctures.

Health and Medical Precautions

The Katy Trail is a relatively safe and well-maintained route, but staying healthy during your trip is critical to ensuring a pleasant experience. Here are some crucial health considerations to bear in mind:

Vaccinations and Medical Check-ups

There are no specific vaccinations required for visiting the Katy Trail, but it's a good idea to be up to date on general vaccinations, especially if you're traveling from abroad. For visitors with medical conditions or those planning longer trips, it's wise to have a medical check-up before embarking. If you require prescription medications, bring enough for the entire trip and keep them easily accessible.

Emergency Preparedness

Know the locations of the nearest medical facilities to where you'll be traveling. In case of emergencies, it's essential to know where to seek help, particularly if you'll be in remote areas. Most towns along the Katy Trail have basic healthcare services, but more serious emergencies may require travel to larger hospitals in cities like Columbia or Jefferson City.

Restrooms and Water Stations

Restrooms are available at most trailheads, but they can be spaced far apart, especially in more remote areas. Water fountains and refill stations are also located at some trailheads, but they are not always available year-round, particularly during winter when pipes may freeze. As a precaution, always carry enough water and plan restroom breaks when passing through towns or well-equipped trailheads.

Local Services and Bike Repair

Several towns along the Katy Trail cater specifically to visitors, offering a range of services, including bike shops, repair stations, and local stores. If you're cycling, many of these shops provide bike rentals, quick repairs, and tools for sale, ensuring you can continue your journey without interruption. Rocheport, St. Charles, and Jefferson City are particularly known for their well-equipped bike repair services, but most larger towns along the trail will have some form of support.

Equipped with practical knowledge of the Katy Trail, you're ready to embark on a safe, enjoyable, and well-prepared journey. Understanding the trail's layout, ensuring safety measures, and having essential gear will enhance your experience, allowing you to focus on enjoying the beauty and adventure that await. Whether you're planning a quick day trip or an extended biking journey, being prepared is the key to making the most of your time on the Katy Trail in 2024-2025.

CHAPTER THREE

Getting There and Around

One of the great advantages of the Katy Trail is its accessibility. Stretching 237 miles through Missouri, this scenic trail is close to several major cities and highways, making it a convenient destination for both local adventurers and visitors from afar. Whether you're driving, flying in from another state, or taking a train, there are plenty of options for getting to the trail and navigating it once you arrive. This chapter will guide you through the various transportation options available, from reaching the trail to exploring the small towns and stunning landscapes that line its route.

Getting to the Katy Trail

By Car

For most visitors, driving is the easiest and most flexible way to reach the Katy Trail. Missouri's extensive highway network makes it simple to access the trail from any direction. The Katy Trail has several key entry points, with some of the most popular located in St. Charles, Clinton, Rocheport, Hermann, and Jefferson City. If you're driving from a nearby state or even from within Missouri, you can pick a trailhead that suits your itinerary and start your adventure with ease.

Major highways such as Interstate 70 (I-70) and U.S. Highway 63 run near the trail, offering easy routes for travelers coming from cities like St. Louis, Kansas City, and Columbia. For example, St. Charles, a popular eastern trailhead, is located just off I-70, making it a convenient starting point for those coming from St. Louis or the surrounding area.

Parking is generally available at most trailheads, although it can vary depending on the location. Larger trailheads, like those in St. Charles and Clinton, offer ample parking facilities, while smaller, rural trailheads may have limited spots. It's worth checking parking availability in advance, especially if you're traveling during peak seasons like spring or fall.

By Plane

For those traveling from further afield, flying into Missouri is a great option. The state is home to several major airports that provide access to the Katy Trail. The closest and most convenient airports are St. Louis Lambert International Airport and Kansas City International Airport.

St. Louis Lambert International Airport (STL)

Located about 10 miles from downtown St. Louis, this airport is the best option for visitors planning to start their journey on the eastern end of the trail. From the airport, you can easily rent a car or take public transportation into St. Charles, which is only a 20-minute drive away.

Kansas City International Airport (MCI)

On the western end of the state, Kansas City International Airport offers easy access to the western trailheads. Clinton, which marks the western terminus of the Katy Trail, is about a 90-minute drive from the airport. Like St. Louis, rental cars are readily available at the airport.

If you're flying in, renting a car is highly recommended for maximum flexibility. Shuttle services from airports to the trail are limited, and many visitors prefer the convenience of having their own vehicle to navigate the towns along the route and access accommodations.

By Train

For those who prefer a more eco-friendly option or want to avoid the hassle of driving, taking the train can be a scenic and convenient way to reach the Katy Trail. "Amtrak's Missouri River Runner", a popular train service running between St. Louis and Kansas City, stops at several towns near the trail, making it a viable option for trail-goers. The following are the train's major stop points:

- **Hermann:** This charming town along the Missouri River is a common stop for Amtrak passengers and provides easy access to the Katy Trail. From the train station, you can reach the trailhead in just a few minutes by car or on foot.

- **Jefferson City:** Another Amtrak stop, Jefferson City is a perfect gateway to the central section of the trail. The trailhead is only a short drive or bike ride from the train station, making it an ideal spot to start your adventure.

The Amtrak service also allows travelers to bring their bikes on board, a major bonus for those planning a biking trip. Be sure to check Amtrak's bike policies and make reservations in advance, as space for bicycles can be limited.

Navigating the Katy Trail

Once you've arrived at the Katy Trail, getting around is part of the adventure. Whether you're exploring by bike, on foot, or using local transportation, the trail is designed to be accessible and easy to navigate. Here's what you need to know about moving between towns and making the most of your time on the trail.

Biking the Trail

Cycling is one of the most popular ways to experience the Katy Trail. Its crushed limestone surface is perfect for hybrid and mountain bikes, and the gentle grade of the trail makes it accessible to riders of all skill levels. The trail's consistent, flat terrain is especially attractive to families and casual riders, while more experienced cyclists will enjoy the longer, more challenging rides.

Bike rentals are available in several towns along the trail, including St. Charles, Rocheport, and Jefferson City. Rental shops often provide bikes, helmets, and gear for both day-trippers and long-distance riders. Some shops even offer delivery services, allowing you to rent a bike in one town and drop it off in another, making one-way rides easy to plan.

If you're bringing your own bike, remember to pack spare tubes, a tire pump, and a basic tool kit for repairs. While the trail is generally well-maintained, punctures and minor mechanical issues can occur, especially in more remote sections.

Hiking the Trail

While cycling is the most common way to explore the Katy Trail, it's also an excellent destination for hikers and walkers. The trail's wide path and well-marked route make it ideal for long hikes or short nature walks. Whether you're looking for a leisurely stroll through scenic landscapes or a multi-day backpacking trip, the Katy Trail offers a variety of options.

For those planning to hike the entire trail, there are plenty of camping spots and accommodations along the way to break up your journey. Be sure to plan your trip with rest stops in mind, as distances between towns can vary, and some sections of the trail are more remote than others.

Local Transportation and Shuttle Services

While the trail itself is non-motorized, several towns along the route offer local transportation options to help visitors get around. If you're planning a longer trip or need assistance with luggage or bike transport, shuttle services are available to make your journey more convenient.

Several companies provide shuttle services that transport cyclists, hikers, and their gear between trailheads and towns. These services can be particularly helpful for those planning a one-way trip, allowing you to ride or hike a section of the trail without worrying about returning to your starting point. Shuttle providers often offer customizable routes, letting you plan pick-up and drop-off points based on your itinerary.

Public transportation is limited in the smaller towns along the trail, but larger towns like St. Charles and

Jefferson City offer taxis and ride-sharing services, making it easier to get around. Rental cars are also available in many of the towns, giving you the freedom to explore nearby attractions beyond the trail.

Parking and Trailhead Access

Parking is generally easy to find at most of the major trailheads, though availability can vary depending on the size of the town and the season. In popular towns like St. Charles, Rocheport, and Clinton, parking lots are spacious and well-maintained, making it easy to leave your car and start your journey.

Smaller, rural trailheads have more limited parking options, so it's worth checking ahead if you're visiting during a busy time. Many trailheads offer free parking, but some of the more developed areas charge a small fee for long-term parking, especially in towns with high tourist traffic.

For multi-day trips, be sure to confirm whether overnight parking is allowed at your starting trailhead. Some towns have specific lots designated for long-term parking, while others may require you to make arrangements with local businesses or accommodations.

Exploring Nearby Towns

One of the most enjoyable aspects of the Katy Trail is the opportunity to explore the quaint towns that dot its path. Each town offers its own unique charm, whether it's the historic sites of St. Charles, the wineries of Hermann, or the riverfront beauty of Jefferson City. These towns provide a welcome respite for travelers, offering places to rest, eat, and explore local culture.

Many towns along the trail are small and easily walkable, making them perfect for a day of sightseeing. Local restaurants, shops, and attractions are typically clustered near the trail, so it's easy to explore without needing additional transportation. For those looking to stay overnight, these towns also offer a range of accommodations, from charming bed-and-breakfasts to boutique hotels and campgrounds.

CHAPTER FOUR

Regions of The Katy Trail

The Katy Trail offers a remarkable variety of landscapes, historical sites, and small-town charm. Each region of the trail has its own unique character and experiences to offer. Whether you're cycling the full length or enjoying a day trip, understanding the distinct regions of the Katy Trail will help you plan an adventure tailored to your interests. In this chapter, we'll break the trail into three primary regions: the Western Section, the Central Section, and the Eastern Section, highlighting what makes each one special.

The Eastern Section: St. Charles to Hermann

SCAN THE QR CODE

The eastern section of the Katy Trail is often considered the most accessible and popular, particularly because it begins in St. Charles, just a short drive from St. Louis. This region is rich in history and filled with picturesque river views, historic towns, and beautiful wineries that line the Missouri River.

Highlights of the Eastern Section

St. Charles

The official starting point of the Katy Trail, St. Charles is a historic city with a charming downtown district. As Missouri's first state capital, it offers plenty of historical attractions, including the First Missouri State Capitol and the quaint, cobblestone streets of Main Street. It's a perfect spot to kick off your adventure, with bike rental shops, restaurants, and lodging options catering to trail-goers.

Augusta

Known for its award-winning wineries, Augusta is a must-visit for wine lovers. The town is nestled in Missouri's wine country, and a stop here offers scenic views of vineyards and rolling hills. It's a great place to relax and enjoy some local flavors after a day of biking or hiking.

Hermann

Another gem of Missouri wine country, Hermann is famous for its German heritage, charming architecture, and annual festivals like Oktoberfest. Visitors can easily spend a day here, sampling wines, exploring historic homes, and enjoying the slower pace of small-town life.

The eastern section is ideal for cyclists and hikers who are interested in combining outdoor adventure with cultural exploration. The relatively short distances between towns make it an excellent choice for day trips or leisurely overnight stays.

The Central Section: Hermann to Rocheport

Moving into the central region, the Katy Trail begins to showcase more of Missouri's natural beauty. This section is known for its towering river bluffs, scenic overlooks, and expansive farmlands. For those looking to connect more deeply with nature, the central region offers some of the most stunning landscapes along the trail.

SCAN THE QR CODE

Highlights of the Central Section

Jefferson City

Missouri's capital city is an interesting stop along the Katy Trail. While the trail itself doesn't run directly through the city, it's just a quick detour across the Missouri River Bridge. In Jefferson City, you'll find the impressive Missouri State Capitol, museums, and local restaurants that give you a taste of Missouri's political and cultural heart.

Rocheport

This small town is often regarded as one of the most scenic and peaceful stops on the trail. The Rocheport area is home to the famous Rocheport Tunnel, an iconic landmark along the Katy Trail, and some of the trail's most dramatic river views. The nearby Les Bourgeois Vineyards offers the perfect spot to enjoy a meal or glass of wine with sweeping views of the Missouri River. Rocheport is also a great place to stay overnight, with charming bed-and-breakfasts and inns.

Katy Trail State Park

The central section also passes through Katy Trail State Park, the longest developed rail-trail park in the country. This park is an excellent place to spot wildlife, enjoy quiet moments of reflection, and absorb the natural beauty that surrounds you.

The central section offers a more secluded experience than the eastern trail, with fewer towns and more focus on Missouri's vast natural beauty. It's perfect for those seeking a peaceful retreat into nature while still enjoying access to the amenities of small towns.

The Western Section: Rocheport to Clinton

SCAN THE QR CODE

The western section of the Katy Trail is the quietest and least traveled, making it ideal for those seeking solitude and a sense of adventure. It's more rural, with long stretches of trail passing through farmlands, forests, and small towns. This region offers a slower, more reflective experience, as it's further removed from the busier cities and tourist hotspots.

Highlights of the Western Section

Sedalia

One of the larger towns in the western region, Sedalia is rich in railroad history and serves as a key point along the trail. The Katy Depot is a must-visit landmark, offering insight into the trail's history and the role of the Missouri-Kansas-Texas Railroad (the "Katy"). Sedalia is also home to the annual Missouri State Fair, so plan your visit around this if you'd like to experience some of the state's local traditions and festivities.

Clinton

The western terminus of the trail, Clinton is a quiet town that marks the end (or beginning) of the Katy

Trail. Though small, Clinton is known for its warm hospitality and makes for a rewarding stop after completing the full length of the trail. Be sure to explore Clinton Square, a charming downtown area with local shops and restaurants.

The western section is ideal for those who want to escape the more developed areas and immerse themselves in Missouri's rural landscape. It's a region best suited for longer, uninterrupted rides or hikes, offering plenty of opportunities for reflection and appreciation of the natural surroundings.

Planning Your Route by Region

When planning your journey along the Katy Trail, understanding the regions helps tailor your experience to match your preferences and time constraints. If you have limited time and want to combine adventure with cultural stops, the eastern section offers quick access to historical towns and wineries. For nature lovers seeking quiet moments of solitude, the central and western sections provide the perfect balance of scenic beauty and peacefulness. No matter which region you explore, the Katy Trail offers an unforgettable journey through the heart of Missouri.

For those seeking a multi-day adventure, consider breaking your trip into segments, allowing time to explore the local attractions in each region. If you're biking the entire trail, you can easily plan overnight stays in towns like St. Charles, Jefferson City, Rocheport, and Sedalia to rest and refuel before continuing on your journey.

Each region of the Katy Trail brings its own charm, history, and beauty to the overall experience. Whether you're drawn to the vibrant wine country of the eastern section, the breathtaking river bluffs in the central region, or the serene farmlands of the western end, the Katy Trail offers a variety of experiences for every traveler. By understanding the unique characteristics of each region, you can plan a trip that aligns perfectly with your interests, making your journey along the Katy Trail a memorable and rewarding adventure.

CHAPTER FIVE

Top Landmarks and Must-see Attractions

The Katy Trail isn't just a beautiful journey through Missouri's countryside—it's a corridor of history, culture, and natural wonders. As you make your way along the trail, there are numerous landmarks and attractions that you simply can't miss. Whether you're interested in Missouri's rich history, stunning river views, or unique local culture, the Katy Trail offers a wealth of fascinating stops along its 237-mile route. In this chapter, we'll take you through the top landmarks and must-see attractions that will make your trip unforgettable.

Katy Depot – Sedalia

A trip to the Katy Trail wouldn't be complete without a visit to the historic Katy Depot in Sedalia. Once a bustling train station, the depot is now a museum that tells the story of the

Missouri-Kansas-Texas (MKT) Railroad, or "Katy", which once ran along what is now the trail. The beautifully restored building showcases exhibits on the region's railroad history, as well as the cultural and economic impact it had on Missouri. It's an ideal first stop to immerse yourself in the history of the trail itself.

Tip: Don't forget to take a picture with the station's iconic railroad car and explore Sedalia's charming downtown before heading back to the trail.

Missouri State Capitol – Jefferson City

Located just off a spur of the Katy Trail, Missouri's State Capitol in Jefferson City is a grand architectural gem that offers visitors a deep dive into the state's history and government. The building itself is a striking example of neoclassical architecture, with stunning marble columns and intricate sculptures. Inside, you'll find the Missouri State Museum, which houses exhibits on the state's cultural and natural history.

The Capitol's location along the Missouri River offers scenic views, making it a great place to take a break from the trail. You can also walk along the city's green spaces or explore Jefferson City's historic downtown area.

Tip: Take a guided tour of the Capitol to fully appreciate the artwork and history, including murals by famed artist Thomas Hart Benton.

Rocheport Bluff and Tunnel

One of the most iconic scenic views along the Katy Trail can be found at Rocheport, where the trail runs alongside towering limestone bluffs and offers sweeping views of the Missouri River. This section is a favorite for both cyclists and hikers, thanks to its dramatic natural beauty. The Rocheport Tunnel, originally constructed in the 1890s for the railroad, adds an extra layer of historical charm to the area.

Rocheport itself is a picturesque small town, perfect for a break. With bed-and-breakfasts, wineries, and cafés, you'll find plenty to do while enjoying the serene river views.

Tip: Time your visit to Rocheport for sunset—the views from the bluffs over the Missouri River are breathtaking as the sun dips below the horizon.

Hermann Wineries and Historic District

Known for its strong German heritage, Hermann is one of the most charming towns along the Katy

Trail. Nestled in the heart of Missouri wine country, Hermann boasts several historic wineries where you can sample locally produced wines and enjoy vineyard tours. Stone Hill Winery and Hermannhof Winery are two of the most popular stops, offering tastings and scenic views of the rolling hills.

Beyond the wineries, Hermann's historic district is filled with well-preserved 19th-century architecture, giving visitors a glimpse into the town's German roots. The annual Oktoberfest draws large crowds, but Hermann's charm is on display year-round, making it an essential stop for history buffs and wine lovers alike.

Tip: Plan your visit around one of Hermann's many festivals, or stop for a relaxing afternoon picnic with a bottle of local wine.

Augusta and the Missouri Wine Country

Another must-see stop along the Katy Trail is the town of Augusta, which is also nestled in Missouri's wine country. As the first federally recognized wine district in the United States, Augusta offers a mix of rich history, fine wine, and small-town charm. Several wineries, including Mount Pleasant Estates and Balducci Vineyards, are located just off the trail, making it easy to enjoy a relaxing day of wine tasting.

The rolling hills and scenic landscapes around Augusta offer some of the most picturesque views along the eastern section of the Katy Trail. After a day of cycling or hiking, the town's tranquil atmosphere makes it an ideal place to unwind.

Tip: Augusta is a perfect destination for a day of wine tasting and cycling—plan your route to visit multiple wineries and enjoy the peaceful beauty of the countryside.

Lewis and Clark Boathouse Center – St. Charles

As the eastern terminus of the Katy Trail, St. Charles is steeped in history, most notably tied to the Lewis and Clark Expedition. The Lewis and Clark Boathouse and Nature Center is located along the Missouri River and offers a fascinating look at the explorers' journey. The museum features full-size replicas of the boats used by Lewis and Clark and exhibits on the wildlife and natural environment they encountered.

Beyond the museum, St. Charles is known for its beautifully preserved Historic Main Street, with cobblestone streets and 19th-century architecture. It's a perfect place to celebrate the end—or beginning—of your Katy Trail adventure with great food, shopping, and history.

Tip: After visiting the museum, stroll through the historic district and enjoy some local cuisine or grab a coffee at one of the many cozy cafés.

Katy Bridge – Boonville

The Katy Bridge in Boonville is a historic landmark and a symbol of the town's connection to the Katy Railroad. This massive steel bridge, which spans the Missouri River, was built in 1932 and is an engineering marvel of its time. While no longer in operation as a railroad bridge, it has been partially restored and opened as a pedestrian and cycling bridge, offering sweeping views of the river and the surrounding landscape.

Boonville itself is a charming town with a rich railroad history, and the bridge stands as a testament to the town's role in Missouri's transportation past. It's a great spot for photos and an ideal stopping point to stretch your legs while taking in the scenery.

Tip: The Katy Bridge is especially beautiful at sunrise or sunset, offering great opportunities for photography and birdwatching.

The Katy Trail is more than just a route for cyclists and hikers—it's a journey through Missouri's natural beauty, history, and culture. From the tranquil bluffs of Rocheport to the bustling historic districts of St. Charles and Hermann, each stop offers something unique to discover. Whether you're a history enthusiast, wine lover, or nature explorer, the Katy Trail's top landmarks and must-see attractions will enrich your adventure and leave lasting memories. So as you plan your trip, be sure to include these incredible stops to make the most of your Katy Trail experience.

CHAPTER SIX

Outdoor Adventure and Experiences

The Katy Trail is much more than a simple cycling or walking path—it's a gateway to a vast range of outdoor adventures and experiences that invite travelers to connect with nature, embrace physical challenges, and explore Missouri's rich natural landscapes. From hiking through scenic river valleys to kayaking alongside towering bluffs, this 237-mile trail offers an abundance of opportunities for outdoor enthusiasts of all kinds. Whether you're seeking solitude in nature or an adrenaline-filled adventure, the Katy Trail is the perfect setting to embark on an unforgettable journey.

Hiking on the Katy Trail

Hiking along the Katy Trail is one of the most accessible and enjoyable ways to experience Missouri's diverse landscapes. The trail offers hikers an opportunity to explore lush forests, open farmland, river bluffs, and wetlands, all in one trip. With relatively flat terrain and well-maintained paths, the Katy Trail is perfect for hikers of all skill levels, from beginners to seasoned trekkers.

Day Hikes

For those looking to enjoy a short, scenic hike, several sections of the Katy Trail are ideal for day trips. One popular area is the stretch near Rocheport, where hikers can walk alongside the majestic Missouri River while enjoying the shade of towering limestone bluffs. Another favored spot is Hermann, where rolling hills and vineyards provide a picturesque backdrop. Shorter hikes along these sections are perfect for families or casual adventurers looking to take in the natural beauty without committing to long distances.

Multi-Day Hikes

If you're ready for a longer hiking adventure, consider planning a multi-day trek along the trail, combining camping or stays in nearby towns. The trail's relatively even grade makes long-distance hiking approachable, and with towns like Boonville, Jefferson City, and St. Charles spaced out along the route, it's easy to find places to rest, grab a bite, and take in local culture. Multi-day hiking trips offer a deeper connection with the natural surroundings, allowing you to slow down and experience the trail's changing landscapes over several days.

Biking the Katy Trail

Cycling is undoubtedly the most popular way to experience the Katy Trail. The trail's hard-packed gravel surface and gentle slopes make it a cyclist's dream, welcoming riders of all ages and skill levels. Whether you're cycling a short section or the entire length of the trail, biking the Katy Trail is an adventure that combines fitness, sightseeing, and exploration.

Day Rides

Many visitors enjoy day rides along various sections of the trail. The central section near Rocheport is a favorite among cyclists, offering scenic views of the Missouri River and a few small hills that add variety without being overly challenging. For a more leisurely ride, the eastern section between Augusta and St. Charles takes riders through Missouri's wine country, with plenty of opportunities to stop at local wineries for a refreshing break.

Long-Distance Cycling

For those looking to embark on a true cycling adventure, the full 237 miles of the Katy Trail provide an epic journey across the heart of Missouri.

Cyclists can plan multi-day trips, staying at cozy bed-and-breakfasts or campgrounds along the route. Popular long-distance itineraries often include stops in Sedalia, Jefferson City, Hermann, and St. Charles, each offering a unique cultural or historical experience. With shuttle services available to transport bikes and gear, planning a longer ride has never been easier.

Wildlife and Bird watching

The Katy Trail is home to an incredible variety of wildlife and is a haven for birdwatchers. The trail's proximity to the Missouri River, as well as the surrounding forests, wetlands, and prairies, make it an ideal habitat for numerous species of birds and animals. Whether you're a dedicated birder or just enjoy observing nature, the Katy Trail offers plenty of opportunities to spot wildlife along the way.

Bird watching

Throughout the year, birdwatchers can expect to see a variety of species, including bald eagles, great blue herons, and songbirds like the indigo bunting. In the spring and fall, migratory birds pass through the area, making it an especially rewarding time for birdwatchers to visit. The wetland areas near Clinton and the river sections near Rocheport are particularly good spots for spotting waterfowl and shorebirds.

Wildlife Viewing

In addition to birds, the trail is home to other wildlife, including deer, wild turkey, raccoons, and beavers. Along the riverbanks, you might even catch sight of an otter swimming or basking on a sunny day. These wildlife encounters, coupled with the tranquil scenery, add a layer of serenity to any outdoor experience on the Katy Trail.

Water Sports and Kayaking

For those looking to complement their hiking or biking adventure with a unique perspective of the Katy Trail, water sports are a fantastic option. The trail runs parallel to the Missouri River for much of its length, offering opportunities for kayaking and canoeing that allow you to experience the landscape from the water.

Kayaking and Canoeing

Several outfitters along the trail, particularly near towns like Rocheport and Jefferson City, offer kayak and canoe rentals, as well as guided river trips. Paddling along the Missouri River allows you to explore areas inaccessible by foot or bike, offering a peaceful and immersive experience surrounded by the beauty of the river valley. These water-based adventures are perfect for cooling off during the warmer months or for travelers looking to experience the trail's natural beauty in a different way.

Fishing

The Missouri River and smaller streams along the trail are also popular spots for fishing. Anglers can try their luck catching catfish, bass, and other species while enjoying the peaceful surroundings. Many trailheads offer easy access to fishing spots, making it convenient to combine a biking or hiking trip with a relaxing day of fishing.

Camping and Overnight Stays

For those seeking a true outdoor adventure, camping along the Katy Trail is an excellent option. Several designated campgrounds are located near trailheads, offering basic amenities like restrooms, picnic areas, and fire pits. Some campgrounds, such as those near Hartsburg and Rocheport, are nestled along the river, providing scenic spots to pitch a tent and fall asleep under the stars.

Camping offers a unique way to connect with the natural surroundings of the Katy Trail, allowing you to enjoy peaceful mornings, wildlife sightings, and the camaraderie of fellow travelers at nearby campsites. It's also a cost-effective option for multi-day adventures, making it easy to extend your trip and explore more of the trail.

The Katy Trail is a paradise for outdoor enthusiasts, offering endless opportunities for adventure and exploration. Whether you're hiking, biking, kayaking, or simply enjoying the peace of nature, the trail invites you to discover the beauty of Missouri's landscapes at your own pace. With its diverse range of outdoor activities, the Katy Trail provides an unforgettable experience for travelers of all kinds, from solo adventurers to families and groups. No matter how you choose to explore, the trail promises a journey filled with discovery, adventure, and lasting memories.

CHAPTER SEVEN

Accommodations Along the Katy Trail

A trip along the Katy Trail isn't just about the journey; where you stay can greatly enhance your experience. The trail winds through charming towns, picturesque countryside, and Missouri's wine country, offering travelers a wide range of accommodations that cater to every type of adventurer. From quaint bed-and-breakfasts and historic inns to campgrounds and riverside cabins, there's no shortage of places to rest, recharge, and enjoy the hospitality of local communities. In this chapter, we'll explore the variety of accommodation options along the Katy Trail, helping you find the perfect stay to suit your needs and preferences.

Bed-and-Breakfasts: A Cozy Retreat

Bed-and-breakfasts (B&Bs) are one of the most popular accommodation choices along the Katy Trail, particularly for cyclists and hikers looking for a warm, comfortable place to rest after a day on the trail. Many B&Bs are housed in historic homes, offering a unique combination of local charm, personal service, and a cozy atmosphere. Guests are typically treated to hearty breakfasts, often featuring local ingredients, and friendly hosts who can provide insider tips on the best places to visit in the area.

Top B&Bs Along the Trail

School House Bed & Breakfast (Rocheport)

A favorite among trail-goers, this historic B&B offers beautifully restored rooms in a former schoolhouse. It's known for its peaceful setting and close proximity to the Missouri River and Rocheport's popular dining and wine-tasting spots.

Captain Wohlt Inn (Hermann)

Nestled in the heart of Missouri's wine country, this charming inn combines history with modern comforts. It's the perfect place for travelers looking to experience Hermann's German heritage and local vineyards.

Glenn House Bed and Breakfast (Boonville)

This stately home offers luxury in a small-town setting. After a long day on the trail, relax in one of the elegant rooms or take a short stroll to nearby attractions like the Katy Bridge.

B&Bs along the Katy Trail offer a unique way to experience Missouri's small towns while enjoying the personal touches that come with locally owned accommodations. Many B&Bs also cater specifically to cyclists, offering bike storage, laundry facilities, and even shuttle services to help guests get back on the trail refreshed and ready for the next leg of their journey.

Hotels and Inns: Comfort and Convenience

For travelers who prefer more traditional accommodations, there are several hotels and inns located in the larger towns along the trail. These options often provide more amenities and services, such as 24-hour check-in, fitness centers, and room service, while still offering easy access to the trail. Hotels are particularly convenient for those who are traveling in groups or looking for a bit more privacy and comfort after a long day outdoors.

Notable Hotels Along the Trail

Hotel Frederick (Boonville)

This historic hotel, originally built in 1905, combines vintage charm with modern amenities. Located right off the trail, it offers beautifully appointed rooms, a full bar and restaurant, and easy access to Boonville's historic downtown area.

The Inn at Defiance (Defiance)

This small but luxurious inn is located in the heart of Missouri's wine country and is ideal for travelers looking to indulge in a bit of comfort. The inn's prime location also makes it easy to explore local vineyards and eateries.

Staying at a hotel or inn along the Katy Trail ensures you'll have a comfortable place to relax after a full day of biking or hiking, with the added benefit of modern conveniences like Wi-Fi, fitness centers, and room service.

Camping: Sleeping Under the Stars

For the outdoor enthusiast, camping along the Katy Trail offers an immersive experience in nature, with the added thrill of sleeping under the stars. Camping is also a budget-friendly option, allowing long-distance travelers to explore more of the trail without breaking the bank. Whether you prefer a tent or a small camper, several campgrounds along the trail cater to cyclists and hikers.

Popular Campgrounds Along the Trail

Katy Roundhouse Campground (New Franklin)

A favorite among cyclists, this well-maintained campground offers tent and RV camping, along with clean facilities and direct access to the trail.

Klondike Park (Augusta)

Located just off the trail, this scenic campground offers tent sites, cabins, and stunning views of the Missouri River valley. It's a peaceful retreat for those looking to escape into nature.

Hartsburg Riverside Campground (Hartsburg)

Situated right by the trail, this rustic campground provides basic amenities and a great location for exploring the charming town of Hartsburg.

Camping along the Katy Trail allows you to experience the full beauty of Missouri's natural landscapes, from the rolling hills to the quiet riverbanks. With several campgrounds offering showers, picnic areas, and fire pits, it's easy to unwind and recharge in the great outdoors.

Unique Stays: Cabins, Cottages, and Guesthouses

For travelers seeking something a little different, there are a number of unique accommodations along the Katy Trail that combine comfort with the charm of the countryside. Whether it's a riverside cabin, a cozy guesthouse, or a vineyard cottage, these options provide a peaceful and secluded retreat while still being close to the trail.

Unique Accommodations Along the Trail

Les Bourgeois Blufftop Cottages (Rocheport)

These cottages, nestled above the Missouri River, offer breathtaking views and easy access to both the trail and the popular Les Bourgeois Vineyards. It's a perfect spot for a romantic getaway or a peaceful retreat.

The Katy Trail Guesthouse (Marthasville)

Located in the heart of wine country, this guesthouse offers the perfect balance of rustic charm and modern amenities. With a full kitchen and spacious rooms, it's ideal for families or groups.

Hermann Hill

For those looking to indulge in luxury, Hermann Hill offers beautiful vineyard views, private hot tubs, and even spa services. It's a wonderful place to relax after a day of riding or hiking.

Unique stays along the Katy Trail offer travelers the chance to unwind in comfort while still enjoying the charm and natural beauty of the region. These accommodations often provide a more intimate experience, perfect for couples, families, or small groups looking for a special stay.

The Katy Trail offers a wide variety of accommodations to suit every traveler's needs, from cozy B&Bs to scenic campgrounds and luxury hotels. No matter how you prefer to rest and recharge, the towns and communities along the trail are ready to welcome you with warm hospitality, beautiful surroundings, and a comfortable place to call home for the night. Whether you're sleeping under the stars or enjoying the luxury of a riverside inn, your stay along the Katy Trail will be an unforgettable part of your adventure.

CHAPTER EIGHT

Food and Drink on The Katy Trail

One of the great joys of traveling the Katy Trail is the opportunity to indulge in Missouri's rich culinary scene. Whether you're refueling after a long day of cycling or savoring the flavors of Missouri's famous wine country, food and drink play a big role in shaping the trail experience. From small-town cafés to local wineries and farmers' markets, the trail offers an array of delicious options for every palate and preference. In this chapter, we'll guide you through some of the best places to eat and drink along the Katy Trail, as well as where to stock up on essentials before continuing your adventure.

Local Cuisine: A Taste of Missouri

Missouri's cuisine reflects its agricultural roots, with an emphasis on hearty, farm-to-table meals that highlight local produce, meats, and flavors. As you travel the Katy Trail, you'll find a mix of down-home comfort food, fresh salads, barbecue, and more, depending on where you stop.

Many restaurants along the trail pride themselves on sourcing ingredients from local farms, giving you the chance to taste the freshest produce and meats available. Classic Midwestern fare such as fried chicken, BBQ ribs, and pork tenderloin sandwiches are easy to find, but so are more refined options like artisanal cheeses, seasonal soups, and fresh vegetables. Whatever your preference, the local cuisine is designed to satisfy hungry adventurers.

Top Eateries Along the Trail

The towns along the Katy Trail are home to some truly wonderful spots for a meal or snack. Here are a few of the best places to stop and refuel:

Abigail's Restaurant (Rocheport)

This local favorite offers a seasonal menu that changes daily, featuring fresh, locally-sourced ingredients. Whether you're craving a hearty lunch or a delightful dinner, Abigail's is known for its creative dishes and friendly service.

Trailside Café (Defiance)

A popular stop for cyclists, Trailside Café serves up classic American fare with a focus on comfort. From hearty breakfast sandwiches to delicious burgers, it's a great place to grab a quick, satisfying bite before hitting the trail again.

Harvest Table (St. Charles)

Located near the eastern terminus of the Katy Trail, Harvest Table offers farm-to-table dishes that celebrate Missouri's agricultural bounty. It's an ideal spot to enjoy a leisurely meal while soaking in the charm of St. Charles' historic district.

Many of these eateries are located close to the trail, making it easy for cyclists and hikers to stop in without straying too far from their journey. Be sure to check local business hours, as some restaurants may have limited opening days or seasonal hours.

Wineries and Breweries: Missouri's Wine Country

No discussion of food and drink on the Katy Trail is complete without mentioning Missouri's famous wine country. The trail passes through some of the state's best vineyards, particularly near Hermann and Augusta, where rolling hills and river valleys provide ideal conditions for winemaking. These wineries are known for producing high-quality varietals like Norton, Chambourcin, and Vidal Blanc, offering trail-goers the perfect way to unwind after a day of exploration. The following are some of the top wineries and breweries along the Katy trail:

Stone Hill Winery (Hermann)

As one of Missouri's oldest and most celebrated wineries, Stone Hill offers tastings and tours of its historic cellars. After a day on the trail, sit back and relax with a glass of their award-winning Norton wine, while taking in views of the surrounding vineyards.

Mount Pleasant Estates (Augusta)

Known for its stunning views and wide selection of wines, Mount Pleasant Estates is another must-visit for those traveling through Missouri wine country. The on-site restaurant also offers delicious, locally-sourced meals to pair with your wine tasting experience.

In addition to wine, Missouri is home to a growing craft beer scene. Breweries like Logboat Brewing Company in Columbia and Trailhead Brewing Company in St. Charles offer unique, locally brewed beers that reflect the character and flavors of the region.

Picnic Spots and Farmers' Markets

Sometimes, the best meal on the Katy Trail is one you create yourself, whether it's a picnic lunch overlooking the Missouri River or fresh fruit from a local farmers' market. Several sections of the trail offer ideal picnic spots where you can enjoy a scenic break while fueling up for the next leg of your journey.

Rocheport Bluff Overlook

This scenic spot, located just outside of Rocheport, offers breathtaking views of the river and bluffs, making it an ideal place to enjoy a packed lunch.

Augusta Park

Located near the town of Augusta, this park features shaded picnic tables and easy access to the trail. It's the perfect place to relax, especially after a visit to one of the nearby wineries.

For those looking to stock up on fresh ingredients, local farmers' markets in towns like Hermann and Boonville offer everything from fruits and vegetables to artisanal cheeses and baked goods. Picking up local produce not only supports the community but also adds fresh flavors to your trail experience.

Hydration and Snacks on the Trail

Staying hydrated and energized is key to enjoying the Katy Trail, especially during the hot summer months. While water fountains are available at some trailheads, it's always a good idea to carry extra water with you, particularly if you're covering long distances between towns.

As for snacks, many of the small stores and cafés along the trail offer trail mix, energy bars, fresh fruit, and other grab-and-go items that will keep you fueled throughout your journey. For those planning longer rides or hikes, consider packing a lightweight cooler with high-protein snacks like nuts, jerky, or cheese to keep your energy levels steady.

Food and drink are an integral part of the Katy Trail experience, from the farm-to-table restaurants and local wineries to the cozy cafés and scenic picnic spots. Whether you're indulging in Missouri's famous wines, sampling local cuisine, or enjoying a simple packed lunch by the river, the trail offers countless opportunities to refuel and savor the flavors of the region. With so many delicious options to choose from, your journey along the Katy Trail will be a feast for both your body and soul

CHAPTER NINE

Festivals, Events and Cultural Highlights

The Katy Trail is more than just a scenic path through Missouri—it's a dynamic route that weaves through a tapestry of festivals, events, and cultural highlights that bring the towns and landscapes along the trail to life. As you journey from one town to the next, you'll find a rich array of local celebrations, historical events, and cultural experiences that deepen your connection to the region. From annual wine festivals to small-town fairs, the Katy Trail offers an opportunity to explore not just the natural beauty of Missouri but also its lively traditions and communities. This chapter will guide you through some of the most engaging festivals, events, and cultural highlights along the trail in 2024-2025.

Oktoberfest (Hermann)

One of the most popular and lively events along the Katy Trail is Oktoberfest in the town of Hermann. Celebrating the area's strong German heritage, Hermann's Oktoberfest is a month-long event that takes place every weekend in October. This festival is a fantastic celebration of traditional German culture, featuring authentic German music, food, dancing, and, of course, beer. Visitors can sample local brews and wines from the nearby vineyards, all while enjoying the festive atmosphere.

Oktoberfest also includes a variety of family-friendly activities, such as wagon rides, craft markets, and guided tours of Hermann's historic district. Whether you're visiting for a day or spending the weekend, this event is a great way to immerse yourself in the local culture while enjoying the beautiful fall colors along the Katy Trail.

Missouri River Irish Fest (St. Charles)

Held annually in St. Charles, the Missouri River Irish Fest is a celebration of Irish culture and heritage in the heart of Missouri. Taking place in May, this three-day festival brings together live Irish music, traditional dance performances, and plenty of food and drink, all with a scenic backdrop of the Missouri River.

Visitors can explore vendor stalls offering handcrafted goods, Celtic jewelry, and Irish-themed merchandise. The festival also features interactive activities like genealogy workshops, where attendees can learn about their Irish roots, and historical exhibits on Irish immigration in Missouri. The Missouri River Irish Fest is a joyful and spirited event, perfect for trail travelers looking to experience something unique while in St. Charles.

Missouri State Fair (Sedalia)

For a true taste of Missouri culture, the Missouri State Fair in Sedalia is a can't-miss event. Held every August, this iconic fair is one of the oldest and largest in the state, attracting visitors from across the region. The fairgrounds come alive with carnival rides, live music, agricultural exhibits, and competitions that celebrate Missouri's farming and rural heritage.

Visitors can stroll through displays of prize-winning livestock, enjoy classic fair foods like funnel cakes and corn dogs, and watch thrilling rodeo performances. The Missouri State Fair also hosts concerts by major national and local acts, making it a great place to catch some live music while enjoying the festive atmosphere. The fair provides an excellent opportunity for trail-goers to experience a slice of traditional Missouri life, all while taking a break from the trail's rural tranquility.

Wine Country Harvest Festival (Augusta)

Missouri's wine country is world-renowned, and the Wine Country Harvest Festival in Augusta is one of the best ways to experience it. Taking place in late September or early October, this festival celebrates the grape harvest with wine tastings, live music, and vineyard tours. Visitors can explore local wineries and sample a wide range of wines, from robust reds to refreshing whites, all while learning about the winemaking process.

The festival also features local food vendors, artisans, and craftspeople, making it a perfect opportunity to indulge in Missouri's culinary and creative arts. With the crisp fall air and vibrant autumn colors providing a stunning backdrop, the Wine Country Harvest Festival is a must-visit event for wine lovers and trail enthusiasts alike.

Christmas Traditions Festival (St. Charles)

St. Charles truly comes alive during the holiday season with its Christmas Traditions Festival, a month-long celebration of all things Christmas. Held from late November through December, this festival transforms the town's historic district into a winter wonderland, complete with carolers in Victorian costumes, horse-drawn carriages, and a festive light display. Visitors can meet holiday characters like Santa Claus, Jack Frost, and Ebenezer Scrooge, all while enjoying seasonal treats and shopping for unique holiday gifts in the charming local boutiques.

The Christmas Traditions Festival is an ideal stop for those looking to experience a bit of holiday magic while exploring the Katy Trail. The festival's warm and welcoming atmosphere, combined with the historic charm of St. Charles, makes it one of the highlights of the holiday season in Missouri.

Art Walks and Farmers' Markets (Various Towns)

In addition to the larger festivals, many of the smaller towns along the Katy Trail host regular events such as art walks and farmers' markets. Towns like Rocheport, Boonville, and Jefferson City often have seasonal markets where visitors can explore fresh produce, local crafts, and handmade goods. These events are a great way to support local farmers and artisans while getting a taste of Missouri's community spirit.

Art walks, often held in towns like Rocheport and Augusta, offer visitors the chance to explore galleries, meet local artists, and purchase unique, handmade pieces. These smaller events give travelers a more intimate glimpse into the cultural life of the communities along the Katy Trail.

The Katy Trail is not just a pathway through nature but a gateway to the vibrant festivals, events, and cultural highlights that define Missouri. From Oktoberfest in Hermann to the Christmas Traditions Festival in St. Charles, there's always something exciting happening along the trail. Whether you're looking to experience the lively atmosphere of a local fair, sip wine during harvest season, or immerse yourself in the music of the region, the Katy Trail provides an endless array of cultural adventures to enhance your journey.

CHAPTER TEN

Suggested Itineraries

Planning the perfect trip along the Katy Trail depends on your interests, available time, and how much of the trail you want to explore. Whether you're looking for a quick day trip, a weekend getaway, or a longer, immersive journey, the trail offers plenty of flexibility for every type of traveler. From scenic riverfront stretches to charming small towns, the Katy Trail has something for everyone. In this chapter, we'll walk through suggested itineraries, from one-day adventures to week-long excursions, offering tailored suggestions for families, solo travelers, and couples alike.

One-Day Adventure: Quick Trail Excursions

If you're short on time but still want to experience the beauty of the Katy Trail, a one-day excursion is a great option. With so many scenic sections to choose from, here are a couple of suggested routes for a day of cycling or hiking.

Option One: Rocheport to McBaine (16 miles round trip)

This section of the trail is one of the most scenic, following the Missouri River and offering stunning views of limestone bluffs. Start in the charming town of Rocheport, where you can grab a coffee at Rocheport General Store before heading out on the trail. As you ride or hike, you'll pass through shady stretches of forest and open vistas of the river, with plenty of spots to stop and take in the scenery. You can make it to McBaine and back in just a few hours, leaving time for lunch at Les Bourgeois Vineyards, where you can enjoy panoramic views of the river while sipping local wine.

Option Two: St. Charles to Defiance (26 miles round trip)

Starting at the eastern end of the trail in St. Charles, this route takes you through the heart of Missouri's wine country. The relatively flat terrain makes it ideal for a leisurely ride or hike, and you'll pass through the town of Defiance, where you can stop for a bite at the Trailside Café. The historic streets of St. Charles offer plenty of post-trail options, from exploring shops and galleries to dining at local restaurants.

Weekend Getaway: Two-Three Day Itineraries for Biking and Hiking

For those with a bit more time, a weekend getaway on the Katy Trail allows you to explore multiple sections of the trail while still enjoying local food, wine, and culture. These itineraries are perfect for a short escape into nature.

Option One: Boonville to Rocheport and Jefferson City (2-3 Days)

Start your weekend in Boonville, a town steeped in railroad history. After exploring the historic Katy Depot Museum, set out on the trail toward Rocheport (12 miles), where you'll be rewarded with beautiful views of the Missouri River. Spend the night at one of Rocheport's cozy bed-and-breakfasts, such as the "School House Bed & Breakfast", and enjoy a meal at "Abigail's" or the vineyard restaurant at Les Bourgeois.

On your second day, continue on to Jefferson City (40 miles), stopping for a break in Hartsburg, a quaint village along the way. Once you arrive in Jefferson City, take time to explore the impressive Missouri State Capitol and unwind in one of the local restaurants.

Option Two: Hermann and Augusta Wine Country (2-3 Days)

For a more relaxed weekend focused on Missouri's wine heritage, start in the historic town of Hermann. Spend your first day exploring the local wineries, such as Stone Hill Winery, and strolling through

Hermann's historic streets. Stay overnight at the charming Captain Wohlt Inn, and enjoy dinner at one of the town's German-inspired restaurants.

On day two, head east on the trail toward Augusta (30 miles). This stretch offers rolling hills and stunning vineyard views, making it one of the most scenic sections of the trail. Stop for lunch and a wine tasting at Mount Pleasant Estates, then spend the night in a local B&B before heading back or continuing your journey.

Week-long Journey: A Seven-Day Immersive Experience

For travelers seeking a deeper, more immersive adventure, a week-long trip along the Katy Trail allows you to experience the full beauty and diversity of Missouri. This itinerary covers the full trail, from Clinton to St. Charles, giving you time to enjoy local attractions and relax along the way.

- **Day One: Clinton to Sedalia (37 miles)**

  Start your journey at the western terminus in Clinton and cycle or hike toward Sedalia.

This section is a peaceful introduction to the trail, passing through farmland and small towns. Spend the night in Sedalia, where you can explore the historic Katy Depot and grab dinner at one of the local restaurants.

- **Day Two: Sedalia to Boonville (36 miles)**

  On day two, continue east toward Boonville. This section includes scenic stretches and some gentle hills. Spend the night at "Hotel Frederick", a beautifully restored historic hotel, and take in the sights of Boonville's charming downtown area.

- **Day Three: Boonville to Rocheport (12 miles)**

  Enjoy a shorter ride on day three as you make your way to Rocheport, one of the most scenic and popular spots along the trail. After arriving, spend the day exploring the town, taking in the river views, and visiting Les Bourgeois Vineyards.

- **Day Four: Rocheport to Jefferson City (40 miles)**
  Prepare for a longer day as you head toward Jefferson City. Along the way, stop in Hartsburg for a quick rest before continuing to Missouri's capital city. Spend the night in Jefferson City, and explore the Missouri State Capitol and local museums.

- **Day Five: Jefferson City to Hermann (43 miles)**
  Day five takes you into Missouri's wine country, with a scenic ride toward Hermann. After a day of cycling, unwind with a wine tasting at Stone Hill Winery and a stay at one of Hermann's welcoming inns.

- **Day Six: Hermann to Augusta (30 miles)**
  This section takes you deeper into the heart of Missouri's wine country. As you travel from Hermann to Augusta, take time to explore the local vineyards and enjoy the beautiful countryside. Spend the night at a

B&B in Augusta, such as "The Lindenhof Bed and Breakfast".

- **Day Seven: Augusta to St. Charles (26 miles)**

  Your final day on the trail takes you from Augusta to St. Charles, the eastern terminus. After arriving, celebrate the end of your journey with a meal in St. Charles' historic district and explore the town's rich history.

Custom Itineraries: Tailored Suggestions for Families, Solo Travelers, and Couples

For Families

Families can enjoy shorter, more manageable sections of the trail, such as the Rocheport to McBaine route, which offers scenic views and an easy ride. Stops at parks, such as Klondike Park near Augusta, provide picnic areas and opportunities for kids to explore nature.

For Solo Travelers

Solo travelers seeking adventure can enjoy a longer ride, such as a Sedalia to Jefferson City trip. This section provides a mix of solitude and small-town charm, with plenty of opportunities to meet fellow travelers at trail stops and local cafés.

For Couples

Couples looking for a romantic getaway will find the Hermann to Augusta stretch perfect for wine tasting and scenic views. Staying overnight at a vineyard B&B and dining at intimate restaurants along the way creates the perfect mix of adventure and relaxation.

The Katy Trail offers a wide range of itineraries for every traveler, from quick day trips to week-long adventures. Whether you're cycling, hiking, or simply enjoying the natural beauty and cultural highlights along the way, these itineraries provide a starting point for planning your perfect Katy Trail experience.

CHAPTER ELEVEN

Sustainable and Responsible Travel

As one of the longest rail-trails in the United States, the Katy Trail not only offers a stunning journey through Missouri's landscapes but also provides a chance for travelers to explore the region in an environmentally responsible way. Whether you're cycling, hiking, or simply enjoying the local communities along the trail, traveling sustainably is key to preserving the natural beauty and cultural richness of the area for future generations.

In this chapter, we'll discuss the importance of sustainable and responsible travel, offer practical tips on how to minimize your impact, and highlight ways to support the local communities that make the Katy Trail experience so special.

Why Sustainable Travel Matters on the Katy Trail

The Katy Trail winds through some of Missouri's most fragile and diverse ecosystems, including wetlands, riverbanks, prairies, and forests. As more people discover the trail's beauty, it's crucial to adopt sustainable travel practices to ensure these landscapes remain healthy and thriving. By being mindful of your environmental footprint, you can help protect wildlife, reduce pollution, and ensure that the trail continues to be a safe and enjoyable space for future travelers.

Sustainable travel is also about giving back to the local communities that rely on tourism for their economic well-being. Many small towns along the trail, from Clinton to St. Charles, benefit from visitors spending money on accommodations, meals, and local goods. By choosing to travel responsibly, you're not only preserving the environment but also helping sustain the livelihoods of those who call these places home.

Tips for Minimizing Your Environmental Impact

- **Leave No Trace**

  One of the simplest and most important principles of sustainable travel is to leave no trace. This means that whatever you bring onto the trail, you take off with you. Whether it's food wrappers, water bottles, or gear, make sure to pack out all of your trash. Litter not only mars the beauty of the trail but can also harm local wildlife. Most trailheads have trash and recycling bins, but it's always a good idea to carry a small bag for waste just in case.

- **Use Reusable Gear**

  Instead of relying on single-use plastic bottles, bring a refillable water bottle or hydration pack with you. Many towns along the trail offer water refill stations, so you can stay hydrated without generating unnecessary plastic waste. Similarly, opt for reusable containers for snacks or meals rather than disposable packaging.

- **Stay on the Trail**

  It can be tempting to venture off the marked path, but doing so can damage fragile ecosystems. The Katy Trail passes through sensitive areas, including wetlands and native plant habitats, which can be easily harmed by foot or bike traffic. By sticking to the designated trail, you help protect these natural environments from erosion and other disturbances.

- **Choose Eco-Friendly Accommodations**

  Many bed-and-breakfasts, hotels, and campgrounds along the trail are adopting eco-friendly practices, such as energy-saving appliances, composting, and recycling programs. When planning your trip, look for lodgings that prioritize sustainability. Not only will you reduce your environmental impact, but you'll also support businesses that are committed to protecting the environment.

- **Reduce Carbon Emissions**

  If possible, minimize your carbon footprint by using public transportation or carpooling to reach the trail. Amtrak's Missouri River Runner service, which stops at towns like Hermann and Jefferson City, offers an eco-friendly way to access the trail while reducing car emissions. Once on the trail, cycling and walking are both zero-emission ways to explore the region.

Supporting Local Communities

Sustainable travel isn't just about protecting the environment—it's also about making a positive impact on the people and places you visit. The Katy Trail passes through many small towns that rely on tourism to support local businesses and artisans. Here's how you can contribute to the well-being of these communities:

Shop and Dine Locally

Rather than stopping at chain restaurants or stores, seek out local businesses along the trail. Small cafés, farmers' markets, and locally-owned shops offer unique products and flavors that you won't find anywhere else. Whether you're picking up a souvenir in Hermann or grabbing lunch in Boonville, spending your money locally helps keep these communities thriving.

Stay in Family-Owned Accommodations

Many of the bed-and-breakfasts and inns along the Katy Trail are family-owned, providing a more personal and unique experience for travelers. By staying in these local establishments, you not only support small business owners but also gain valuable insights into the history and culture of the area.

Participate in Local Events

The towns along the Katy Trail often host seasonal festivals, markets, and cultural events. Participating in these activities not only enriches your travel experience but also helps sustain the local economy.

Whether it's attending Oktoberfest in Hermann or joining a summer farmers' market in Hartsburg, these events provide an opportunity to engage with the community and support local artisans, farmers, and entertainers.

Respecting Wildlife and Local Culture

The Katy Trail is home to a wide range of wildlife, from deer and wild turkey to migratory birds and native plants. To ensure these species thrive, it's important to respect their habitats and avoid any disruptive behaviors.

Observe Wildlife from a Distance

While it's exciting to spot wildlife along the trail, it's crucial to maintain a respectful distance. Avoid feeding animals, as human food can be harmful to them, and always give wildlife plenty of space to move freely. Keep your pets on a leash and under control to prevent them from disturbing local wildlife.

Learn About Local Culture and History

Each town along the Katy Trail has its own unique history and culture. Take time to visit local museums, historic sites, and cultural landmarks. Understanding the history of these communities enriches your travel experience and fosters a deeper appreciation for the places you're exploring. From the Missouri State Capitol in Jefferson City to the First Missouri State Capitol Historic Site in St. Charles, the trail offers numerous opportunities to connect with Missouri's heritage.

Traveling sustainably and responsibly on the Katy Trail not only enhances your experience but also ensures that future generations can enjoy the same natural beauty and cultural richness. By following sustainable practices—such as leaving no trace, supporting local businesses, and respecting wildlife—you contribute to the preservation of Missouri's landscapes and communities. Whether you're hiking, cycling, or simply enjoying the journey, making mindful choices will leave a positive impact long after your adventure on the Katy Trail ends.

CHAPTER TWELVE

Insider Tips and Local Secrets

The Katy Trail is packed with well-known attractions, stunning scenery, and charming small towns, but part of what makes the journey special is discovering its hidden gems and local secrets. Whether you're a seasoned traveler or a first-time visitor, there are plenty of lesser-known spots and tips that can elevate your experience. From secret picnic spots to insider advice on the best times to ride, this chapter will guide you through the local secrets that make the Katy Trail truly unforgettable.

Best Time to Hit the Trail

While the Katy Trail is beautiful year-round, timing can make a big difference in your experience. Spring and fall are widely endorsed as the best times to visit. In spring, the trail bursts to life with wildflowers and pleasant temperatures, making it ideal for both hiking and cycling. Fall brings cooler temperatures and beautiful foliage, especially in areas like Rocheport, where the river bluffs are covered in reds, oranges, and yellows.

To avoid crowds, plan your trip for weekdays or early mornings. While popular sections like Rocheport and St. Charles can get busy on weekends, early risers will often find the trail quiet and peaceful, with prime opportunities for wildlife spotting.

Hidden Picnic Spots

The Katy Trail offers plenty of well-known spots to rest and refuel, but there are also a few hidden gems where you can enjoy a quiet, scenic picnic away from the crowds. One such spot is the Bluff

Overlook near Rocheport. Just a short walk or ride off the trail, this overlook offers sweeping views of the Missouri River and the surrounding countryside. It's the perfect spot to relax, enjoy lunch, and take in the tranquility of nature.

Another lesser-known picnic spot is Tebbetts Shelter, located between Jefferson City and Mokane. This shelter offers a peaceful rest area with picnic tables and shade, making it a great stop for cyclists covering longer distances.

Stay at Unique Accommodations

While the towns along the Katy Trail are filled with charming bed-and-breakfasts and inns, some unique accommodation options provide a more memorable experience. For a one-of-a-kind stay, consider booking a night at the "Katy Trail Grand Bunkhouse" in Tebbetts. This simple, hostel-style bunkhouse caters specifically to cyclists and offers a comfortable, affordable overnight option with plenty of camaraderie.

For a more luxurious stay, check out "Les Bourgeois Blufftop Cottages" in Rocheport. These cottages are nestled above the Missouri River, offering breathtaking views and easy access to Les Bourgeois Vineyards, where you can enjoy wine tastings and gourmet meals with a view.

Wineries Off the Beaten Path

Missouri's wine country is a major draw for Katy Trail travelers, and while famous wineries like Stone Hill Winery in Hermann are certainly worth a visit, there are several smaller, lesser-known vineyards that offer a more intimate experience. "Adam Puchta Winery", located just outside of Hermann, is the oldest continuously owned family winery in the United States and offers a quiet, rustic atmosphere perfect for relaxing after a day on the trail.

In "Defiance", be sure to visit "Noboleis Vineyards", a family-owned winery that offers beautiful vineyard views, wine tastings, and plenty of outdoor space to unwind. The winery is close to the trail, making it a convenient stop for a mid-ride break or a leisurely afternoon.

Shuttle and Bike Repair Services

One of the most useful local secrets for long-distance cyclists is the availability of shuttle services along the trail. Several local businesses offer shuttle options, allowing you to bike one way and then get a ride back to your starting point. Katy Bike Rental in Defiance is one such service that offers both bike rentals and shuttle services for trail-goers, making it easier to plan out longer rides without backtracking.

If you run into any bike troubles while on the trail, don't worry—many towns offer bike repair services and rental options. One insider tip is to check out Red Wheel Bike Shop in Jefferson City, known for its quick repairs and friendly staff who can get you back on the trail in no time.

Local Food and Drink Recommendations

While the Katy Trail is known for its wineries, don't miss out on some of the local eateries that offer delicious, home-cooked meals. For breakfast, locals recommend "Dotty's Café" in Hartsburg, a small diner famous for its hearty meals and welcoming atmosphere. For a sweet treat, stop by The Katy Trail Ice House in St. Charles, where you can cool down with ice cream or enjoy a cold beverage on their outdoor patio.

The beauty of the Katy Trail lies not only in its landscapes and attractions but also in the hidden gems and local experiences that many travelers overlook. By venturing off the beaten path, taking advantage of insider tips, and seeking out unique spots along the trail, you can create a truly personalized and unforgettable adventure. Whether it's a secret picnic spot or a cozy bunkhouse stay, the local secrets of the Katy Trail will leave you with lasting memories and a deeper appreciation for Missouri's natural beauty and dynamic communities.

CHAPTER THIRTEEN

Travel Resources and Additional Information

Planning a successful trip along the Katy Trail is made easier with the right resources at your fingertips. Whether you're a first-time visitor or a seasoned traveler, having access to reliable information, maps, and tools will ensure a smooth and enjoyable experience. This chapter provides an overview of key travel resources, apps, websites, and additional tips that will help you make the most of your Katy Trail adventure.

Katy Trail State Park Official Website

The official Katy Trail State Park website is your go-to resource for up-to-date trail conditions, maps, and park information. The site provides a comprehensive trail map with detailed information on trailheads, mileage, and amenities, making it easy to plan your route. It also offers updates on trail closures or repairs, ensuring you stay informed about any detours or conditions that could affect your journey. Whether you're biking, hiking, or just exploring the towns along the trail, this website is a valuable resource.

Website: [Katy Trail State Park] (https://mostateparks.com/park/katy-trail-state-park)

Interactive Trail Maps and Apps

Several apps and websites offer interactive maps and navigation tools to enhance your trail experience. These tools provide real-time information on your location, nearby points of interest, and trail amenities. Some of the top interactive trail maps and apps include:

- **TrailLink:** The TrailLink app by Rails-to-Trails Conservancy is a fantastic resource for finding detailed maps of the Katy Trail. The app provides GPS-enabled maps, reviews from other travelers, and information on rest stops, parking, and more.

- **Ride with GPS:** If you're a cyclist, the "Ride with GPS" app offers customizable route planning and turn-by-turn navigation, ensuring you never get lost on the trail. This app allows you to download maps for offline use, which is especially handy in areas with limited cell service.

- **AllTrails:** The "AllTrails" app is popular among hikers and offers trail reviews, maps, and the ability to track your progress. You can also download maps for offline use, making it a great resource for both short and long hikes along the Katy Trail.

Local Visitor Centers and Tourism Offices

Throughout the Katy Trail, several towns have visitor centers and tourism offices that provide valuable local information, maps, and recommendations. These centers are staffed by locals who can offer insider tips, suggest nearby attractions, and help you find lodging or dining options. Some of the best visitor centers include:

- **St. Charles Visitor Center:** A great resource for travelers starting or ending their journey at the eastern terminus.

- **Jefferson City Visitor Center:** Offers helpful guidance for exploring Missouri's capital and nearby trail sections.

- **Boonville Welcome Center:** Located near the center of the trail, providing maps and insights into the town's rich history.

Emergency Contacts and Health Resources

Before setting out on the trail, it's important to be prepared with emergency contact information. Many sections of the Katy Trail pass through rural areas with limited services, so knowing where to find help is essential.

- **Emergency Numbers:** Dial 911 for any urgent medical or safety concerns.

- **Missouri State Parks Emergency Line:** For non-life-threatening issues on the trail, you can contact the Missouri State Parks emergency line at (800) 334-6946.

Bike Rentals and Repair Shops

Several towns along the trail offer bike rental services and repair shops, ensuring you're always prepared for the next leg of your journey. Notable locations include:

- **Katy Bike Rental (Defiance):** Offers rentals, repairs, and shuttle services.

- **Red Wheel Bike Shop (Jefferson City):** Known for quick repairs and friendly service.

- **The Bike Stop Café (St. Charles):** Provides rentals, snacks, and bike repairs right on the trail.

From interactive maps to local visitor centers and emergency contacts, these travel resources will ensure your Katy Trail adventure is well-planned and enjoyable. By using these tools and staying informed, you can focus on the beauty and charm of Missouri's most famous trail, knowing you have everything you need for a safe and unforgettable journey.

CONCLUSION

The Katy Trail offers more than just a journey through the heart of Missouri—it provides a unique experience where history, nature, and culture come together to create unforgettable memories. From the towering river bluffs and serene farmlands to the charming small towns rich with local heritage, the Katy Trail is a treasure waiting to be explored. Whether you're a casual day-tripper, an avid cyclist, or someone seeking a week-long adventure, this trail has something for everyone.

As you've seen throughout this guide, the Katy Trail is more than just a recreational path. It's a vibrant, living route that connects communities, celebrates Missouri's history, and offers a wide variety of outdoor experiences. From exploring scenic picnic spots and hidden gems to participating in local festivals and supporting small businesses, your journey on the trail is a chance to immerse yourself in the best that Missouri has to offer.

As you plan your 2024-2025 Katy Trail adventure, keep in mind the principles of sustainable and responsible travel to ensure that this beautiful route remains intact for generations to come. Whether you're hiking, biking, or enjoying the local culture, this guide has equipped you with the tools and insider tips to make the most of your trip.

So, lace up your hiking boots, hop on your bike, and get ready to embark on a journey filled with discovery, beauty, and unforgettable memories. Your adventure awaits—enjoy every step of the way!

Made in the USA
Coppell, TX
11 December 2024

42229870R00085